Lessons from Jonah

Pastor Al Stewart

PoBoy Publishing © 2023

All quotations, notes, and articles are mentioned with the source right at the time of usage. *(Any links provided were in operation at the time of this release)* Thus, there is no need for a bibliography. All websites and articles mentioned at the time of this publication were accurate, but are subject to change in the future or may cease to exist. The listing and mentioning of these sites or articles does not imply publisher endorsement of the sites entire contents.

Printed in the United States

Library of Congress IBSN: 9798844162121

Table of Contents

Introduction

There is perhaps no other book in the entire Bible that I have enjoyed teaching from than the book of Jonah.

There is so much to be learned from this incredible book. In it we learn great examples about the character of God. We learn who He is and what His desires are, as well as seeing His nature all throughout, especially in the final chapter. We also see the following play out, His incredible love for all people, no matter how lost they are. *(If you know anything about the Ninevites, then you know just how lost they were!)* And He lives up to this well-known saying, *"He is the God of second chances."*

In short, there is so much to glean from this book. We will see how running from God only makes things worse, or how our actions can and will affect those around us; something I think we overlook when making decisions, conversely we also see how God moves when we are obedient, and we see the great result of remaining faithful in the midst of trials. Last, we'll see that God takes notice when we take the proper action. So friends, come along on this journey with me as we dig into this wondrous book. My heartfelt prayer is that when you finish your study and reading here, your love for God will be that much deeper, and your ability to trust Him at all times will flourish!

Pastor Al Stewart,

1/17/23 – 4:20 pm.

Chapter 1

The Beginning of Troubles

The book of Jonah opens with this statement....

Jonah 1:1: The word of the Lord came to Jonah son of Amittai: (CSB Bible)

The first thing we learn is that we need to be ready and obedient when the word of the Lord comes to us! Consider what Jonah said to God as we quickly skip ahead to chapter four......

Jonah 4:2: He prayed to the Lord, "Please, Lord, isn't this what I said while I was still in my own country? That's why I fled toward Tarshish in the first place. I knew that you are a gracious and compassionate God, slow to anger, abounding in faithful love, and one who relents from sending disaster. (CSB Bible)

We get the sense that Jonah kind of knew this *"call"* from God was coming. And it seems he even knew what the final results were going to be! Something that he absolutely with all his being did not want to see happen! So what did he do, obey, pack his bags and head to Nineveh? Well, Jonah did pack his bags, but instead he headed to Tarshish, a well-known resort place at the time. I assume Jonah figured he'd get in some R&R and go lay in the sun on the beach instead of obeying God. So let's talk about our first deep truth we learn here. Running from God **NEVER** pays off! The Psalmist gives us great advice in:

Psalm 139:7-12: Where can I go to escape your Spirit? Where can I flee from your presence? 8 If I go up to heaven, you are there; if I make my bed in Sheol, you are there. 9 If I fly on the wings of the dawn and settle down on the western horizon, 10 even there your hand will lead me; your right hand will hold on to me. 11 If I say, "Surely the darkness will hide me, and the light around me will be night"—

12 even the darkness is not dark to you. The night shines like the day; darkness and light are alike to you. (CSB Bible)

As we've just read running from God is futile. The truth is that we may be able to run, but we can never hide from God or His Holy Spirit as we've just read. Elsewhere in Scripture we are told that *"our sin will surely find us out."* Think about it, isn't it true that we run away or hide somewhere pretty much only when we are in sin?

Another deep truth we learn about running is that you can guarantee that a **calamity of some sort is going to follow**, I'm sorry to say this, but running or hiding only compounds the situation. I remember back in 1977 when things we not going very well for me I enlisted in the Army. When I met my recruiter he asked me where I'd like to go, my response was, *"what's the farthest place available?"*

So I packed up and headed to what was West Germany at the time figuring it was a LONG way from home and I'd leave all my problems far behind, however I had this sense that when my plane landed, another landed shortly after, and that one was carrying all my problems! Yes, we can run, but we can't hide this is why Psalm 46:10 is GREAT counsel when things begin to go *"off the rails."* Just listen to this powerful verse.

Psalm 46:10: "Stop fighting, and know that I am God, exalted among the nations, exalted on the earth." (CSB Bible) Your Bible may say *"cease striving."* The idea here in this verse is one of a man whose arms are up in a defensive posture. God is saying in essence, *"go ahead and just put those arms down!"* There's no better time to stop and contemplate then when are you planning on running.

Okay, I said that when we run calamity waits, and that is exactly what happened to Jonah. Things did indeed get worse. Let's pick up the text in chapter one at verse four. Jonah has now boarded this boat headed for Tarshish.

Jonah 1:4-7: But the Lord threw
a great wind onto the sea, and
such a great storm arose on the
sea that the ship threatened to
break apart. 5 The sailors were
afraid, and each cried out to his
god. They threw the ship's cargo
into the sea to lighten the load.
Meanwhile, Jonah had gone
down to the lowest part of the
vessel and had stretched out
and fallen into a deep sleep. 6
The captain approached him and
said, "What are you doing sound
asleep? Get up! Call to your god.
Maybe this god will consider us,
and we won't perish." 7 "Come

on!" the sailors said to each other. "Let's cast lots. Then we'll know who is to blame for this trouble we're in." So they cast lots, and the lot singled out Jonah.

Remember what I said about your sin finding you out? It may even happen while you are asleep in the bottom of a ship completely out of sight! I still wonder how that lot found him. I can just picture that person dropping one down next to him as he laid there sleeping all alone. Its pretty clear that God has no trouble finding us no matter where we are.

Chapter 2

How many will you take with you?

We are in Jonah chapter one having just looked at verses four through seven. What we are about to see is perhaps the **most sobering personal lesson ever taught in Scripture.** So as my friend and outstanding Bible teacher Joe Stowell always states, *"I need you all to be in right now!"*

Let's pick up the text in verse eight to see this profound lesson from God's word.

Jonah 1:8-15: Then they said to
him, "Tell us who is to blame for
this trouble we're in. What is
your business, and where are
you from? What is your country,
and what people are you from?"
9 He answered them, "I'm a
Hebrew. I worship the Lord, the
God of the heavens, who made
the sea and the dry land." 10
Then the men were seized by a
great fear and said to him, "What
have you done?" The men knew
he was fleeing from the LORD's
presence because he had told
them. 11 So they said to him,
"What should we do to you so
that the sea will calm down for
us?" For the sea was getting
worse and worse.

12 He answered them, "Pick me up and throw me into the sea so that it will calm down for you, for I know that I'm to blame for this great storm that is against you."
13 Nevertheless, the men rowed hard to get back to dry land, but they couldn't because the sea was raging against them more
and more. 14 So they called out to the Lord, "Please, Lord, don't let us perish because of this man's life, and don't charge us with innocent blood! For you, Lord, have done just as you
pleased." 15 Then they picked up Jonah and threw him into the sea, and the sea stopped its raging. (CSB Bible)

Did you catch it?

Everything in this text tell me that if they did not toss Jonah off the boat, it was going to sink! Now consider that there had to be at the very least a few hundred people on that boat, perhaps even as many as five hundred. Thus, let's consider that startling truth. **One man's sin was about to take a few hundred uninvolved, now involved people with him all the way to the bottom of the ocean!**

Let's make this personal.......when was the last time you made a bad decision or did something that ended up causing others to be hurt? Did you stop to think of the consequences your actions would have on those around you? Just imagine for a moment if a husband before cheating on his wife thought of the impact his actions would have upon his children. Or if a businessman considering embezzling from his company first stopped to contemplate what will happen to his family should he get caught?

Unlike Jonah's predicament, those two situations are not really about "*life or death.*" One of the wildest stories I ever heard came from a friend of mine from many years ago. He told me that he was addicted to gambling and it got so bad that one night while playing poker in his basement, he gambled away his house, **yes his house!** He begged the man, a man by the way he told me that was *"connected"* if you know what I mean, to please allow him play one last hand to win his house back or literally move out in the morning and hand this guy the keys, can you imagine that? And all the while his wife and children were sound asleep upstairs never realizing what was going on in the basement game room.

My friend told me he went into the bathroom before that final hand and got on his knees and for the first time in his life, despite being a devout Roman Catholic at the time begged God for mercy and prayed with much fear and trembling, sort of the way Jonah prayed in the belly of the sea creature as we'll read later. Well by God's grace he won the hand and his house was saved.

And I'm happy to say that he also told God that if He delivered him in this last hand that he'd serve him. I know this story because this man and his family became a part of our Church a few years later. Thankfully he obeyed God and followed through to commit his life and his family to the Lord. Glory be to the name that is above every name, the name of Jesus, Amen and Amen. Ok back to the text here in Jonah. It's obvious that these people were definitely going to lose their lives due to **one man's sin**. *(Anyone here thinking of Adam and Eve?)*

I have to admit that this came as a real wake up call to me. For I certainly know I have failed a few times in my life and those times were definitely followed by negative consequences. But I don't know if I ever really considered that many people around me would be affected. I'm thankful that I do realize that now. May God help you and me going forward to consider Jonah here before we *"run"* or do something foolish, by considering the outcome to those loved ones around us Amen.

Chapter 3

The Sea Creature

What do you mean by sea creature, don't you mean whale? No I don't. Now I'm not going to get into the argument of whether a whale can actually shallow a man, *(you can go on the internet and find all kinds of stories, most of which seem to be unsubstantiated!)* and have him live for 3 days and nights in his belly. The reason is because I don't believe it was your typical whale. I believe it was a creature made by God especially for this event. I may be wrong here, but that's what I sense here as the scripture says that God *"appointed"* this fish to swallow Jonah. I read. And it shouldn't be too difficult for us as Christians to trust that God can make a specific fish for this lone event Amen! Here's what we read about this creature in chapter one.

Joshua 1:17: The Lord appointed a great fish to shallow Jonah, and Jonah was in the belly of the fish three days and three nights. (CSB Bible) Jesus used this event when talking to the Pharisees who were always seeking after a sign. The Hebrew word for appointed here when transliterated into English is: *"mānâ"* which can mean to prepare as in the Lord prepared a specific sea creature for this event. It can also mean to allot. As I stated, I believe that the Lord made a very specific creature to swallow Jonah and hold him for those three days and nights.

Now sadly by saying whale all the time, millions have come to believe that this story, **which I fully believe did happen,** is merely a fairytale of sorts or a story that has an important lesson, but didn't actually take place. To believe that this event didn't take place is to put one in conflict with Jesus own words about Jonah found in Matthew 12:38-42.

Matthew 12:38-41: Then some of the scribes and Pharisees said to him, "Teacher, we want to see a sign from you." 39 He answered them, "An evil and adulterous generation demands a sign, but no sign will be given to it except the sign of the prophet Jonah. 40 For as Jonah was in the belly of the huge fish three days and three nights, so the Son of Man will be in the heart of the earth three days and three nights.

41 The men of Nineveh will stand up at the judgment with this generation and condemn it, because they repented at Jonah's preaching; and look —

something greater than Jonah is here. (CSB Bible)

I can't imagine that Jesus would use for an illustration a story that never took place! As a side note many people say the same thing about Noah and the Ark or even the flood. And since Jesus used Noah as an illustration as well, I'd say with confidence that we can believe that that event also took place.

Chapter 4

Giving thanks when things aren't going well

Jonah is swallowed up by the mighty sea creature that I believe God made especially for this event. Picking up the text in chapter two, we read Jonah's prayer:

Jonah 2:1-10: Jonah prayed to the Lord his God from the belly of the fish: 2 I called to the Lord in my distress, and he answered me. I cried out for help from deep inside Sheol; you heard my voice. 3 When you threw me into the depths, into the heart of the seas, the current overcame me.

*All your breakers and your
billows swept over me. 4 And I
said, “I have been banished from
your sight, yet I will look once
more toward your holy temple.”
5 The water engulfed me up to
the neck; the watery depths
overcame me; seaweed was
wrapped around my head. 6 I
sank to the foundations of the
mountains, the earth’s gates
shut behind me forever! Then
you raised my life from the Pit,
Lord my God!*

*7 As my life was fading away, I
remembered the Lord, and my
prayer came to you, to your holy
temple. 8 Those who cherish
worthless idols abandon their
faithful love,* ***9 but as for me, I***

will sacrifice to you with a voice of thanksgiving. I will fulfill what I have vowed. Salvation belongs to the Lord. *10 Then the Lord commanded the fish, and it vomited Jonah onto dry land.* (CSB Bible)

This kind of reminds me of the Psalmist in Psalm 73. For most of that Psalm the tone is pretty bleak. The Psalmist wonders how it is that evil people so often seem too prosper in this life, but like Jonah here he awakens to the truth. Another merciful truth about God is that although Jonah was rebellious and resistant to His plan, He still sought to save and use Him. Isn't it good to know friends that when we go astray, the Lord doesn't go away! Yes! He really is the God of the second chance.

So now we see our friend Jonah stuck in this sea creature with three days to think about it......that's a long time! But notice verses eight through ten. He awakens and take note that he does so NOT after things start getting better, an important principle for us to learn, but he awakens right in the middle of his calamity! Friends when was the last time you found your *"Praise"* in the middle or during the storm? Did you wait for it to pass to be thankful? I truly believe this is something very important because so many believers over the years have missed great opportunities due to giving up prematurely.

Consider Galatians 6:9: *Let us not get tired of doing good, for we will reap at the* ***proper time if we don't give up.*** (CSB Bible)

Take note of the last seven words. God has a *"proper"* time for us to arise out of a situation, but **ONLY** if we don't grow weary and give up. Jonah didn't so now let's watch how God turned the tide in the next chapter, something by the way He is renowned for.

Chapter 5

The God who turns the tide!

We are now in chapter three as Jonah's prayer took up all of chapter two. Let's pick up the text in verse one.

Jonah 3:1-3: The word of the Lord came to Jonah a second time: 2 "Get up! Go to the great city of Nineveh and preach the message that I tell you." 3 Jonah got up and went to Nineveh according to the LORD's command. Now Nineveh was an extremely great city, a three-day walk. (CSB Bible)

As soon as we learn as Jonah to be thankful and to trust **IN** the middle of our calamity not afterwards when it's safe, please notice what follows.......*"The word of the Lord came a second time."* God will begin to speak again! To that there can be no question; the real test however is whether or not we will be listening when it comes the second time.

And hopefully like our friend Jonah we will be obedient and will respond not just in word, but also with action. I am reminded of that old favorite Baptist Hymn, *"Trust and Obey, for there is no other way."* Pay close attention to the fact that Jonah got up and obeyed the Lord and started his three day trek to Nineveh, albeit it may have been grudgingly, but none the less, he obeyed and God is always pleased when we obey Him friends!

This is where I want to thank Pastor Nate Buker. My inspiration to continue this book was really due to him and I'll explain. When we moved to Florida in late 2021, in early 2022 I launched a local weekly Pastors group, something I've done everywhere I've lived. And around May of 2022 at that local Pastor's meeting I was challenged by something Pastor Nate said that sparked my desire to restart this project. In fact, it was something that in all my study of Jonah I had never thought about and certainly never would have had I not heard what he said. Each week at our group we have a different person do the *"devo"* or devotional which is just a short word that we all talk about afterwards. That particular morning it was my turn. I talked about the book of Jonah and when we got to the part where we are now in this book Nate said the following that literally, to use a term from my generation *"blew me away."* He said ***"can you just imagine for a moment the kind of preaching Jonah must have delivered? Seems to me since he wasn't***

happy, he probably blasted those people! I'm quite sure it wasn't the most positive preaching we've ever heard."

Now that may not seem like much to you, but to me it was something I'd never thought about. The fact that Jonah was so displeased with God and frankly was downright angry as Pastor Nate said, had to have reflected in some way in his preaching to the Ninevites. And yet God still used him regardless of whatever his preaching style was! Was it due to his obedience, albeit as I mentioned earlier grudgingly?

Only God knows that answer, but what a great lesson friends

to learn that when we are obedient, especially when we don't like it or understand it, God still shows up! It's almost comical in my mind to think about Jonah preaching halfheartedly and shouting at the Ninevites, but God sure used it!

Thank you Pastor Nate!

Chapter 6

Leave the results to God

I once saw a meme that pictured a man looking intently around the corner as though he was spying on someone. The caption read, *"Me, checking in on God to make sure He does what He said He'll do!"* Trusting and then obeying God will lead us right into this next deep truth.

God will do what He set out to do! Now while it is 100% true that God doesn't always get what He wants or desires. *(I could site many facts such as what we are told in 1 Tim. 2:4 that God desires all men* *(mankind) to be saved. However, this clearly isn't happening)*

But when God sets out to do a very specific thing like what He desired to do in Nineveh, you can definitely *"take it to the bank."* We can have full confidence that whatever He wanted in a particular situation is going to happen! And sure enough when Jonah preached, *(regardless of the style of his preaching)* the people from the King all the way down responded as follows.

Jonah 3:4-10:Jonah set out on the first day of his walk in the city and proclaimed, "In forty days Nineveh will be demolished!" 5 Then the people

of Nineveh believed God. They
proclaimed a fast and dressed in
sackcloth — from the greatest of
them to the least. 6 When word
reached the king of Nineveh, he
got up from his throne, took off
his royal robe, covered himself
with sackcloth, and sat in ashes.
7 Then he issued a decree in
Nineveh: By order of the king
and his nobles: No person or
animal, herd or flock, is to taste
anything at all. They must not eat
or drink water.

8 Furthermore, both people and
animals must be covered with
sackcloth, and everyone must
call out earnestly to God. Each
must turn from his evil ways and
from his wrongdoing. 9 Who

knows? God may turn and relent; he may turn from his burning anger so that we will not perish.
10 God saw their actions — that they had turned from their evil ways — so God relented from the disaster he had threatened them with. And he did not do it. (CSB Bible)

Now ultimately history sadly tells us that they did perish some seventy or so years later, but at this time God had mercy on them. And keep this in mind. These Assyrians *(Nineveh was the capital of Assyria)* were not nice people. There are graphic accounts of their cruel treatment of captives found in the Assyrian records. The Ninevites were well-known for their savagery in plundering cities. When the Ninevites conquered a nation they would torture and murder in cold-blood. They were known to burn boys and girls alive and torture adults sometimes tearing the skin from their bodies and leaving them to die in the scorching sun!

Rather than hide such depravity they actually celebrated and proclaimed it! Even building monuments to their own cruelty! And yet despite all this somehow God still had mercy upon them. I think of our nation in 2023. Many actually celebrate abortion as a birth control method; we celebrate many things that God speaks clearly against. I can't help but to think of the Prophet Isaiah who spokes these poignant words.

Isaiah 5:20: Woe to those who call evil good and good evil, who substitute darkness for light and light for darkness, who substitute bitter for sweet and sweet for bitter.

I have had many conversations over the last few years with believers from all over who all wonder the same thing. *"How long will God put up with our sin before He says enough is enough?"* I don't know that answer, but I fear for our Nation more today than I ever have before.

Chapter 7

God responds to Action

There's a lot I could write in this chapter about how God responds to action. In one of my other books, *"The Importance of Just One Revisited"* I talk at length about one thing........consistency, as well as being obedient. I believe they go hand in hand. There is a passage of Scripture that is often overlooked, but let's take a close peak at it here.

James 4:8a Draw near to God, and he will draw near to you. (CSB Bible)

Have you ever stopped to think why it was written this way? Notice whom approaches whom! This passage tells us that God is obviously not from the state of Missouri. *(Although He certainly loves it!)* Their motto is: "*the show me state.*" But with God it's different, it's like one of my former mentors in the Lord, Bob Cronk taught me many, many years ago. ***"Man says show me and I'll believe," God says "believe and I'll show you!"***

I say all that to say this......when we take action or any kind of step of obedience, I believe the Scriptures teach that God begins to move on our behalf, in other words, He takes notice, and He does so because He is pleased with our act of obedience. The Bible has a lot to say about obedience and being consistent. Just do a word search and you will see what I mean. And the best Scripture that teaches consistency and how much God will bless it is Matthew 6:33. Last, let's look at some of the best ways we can draw near to God via action/obedience.

In Jonah's case it was to be obey God even if grudgingly. Maybe God has been speaking to you about stepping out or up in some way, but you've been hiding? Or perhaps you've felt His tug to speak to a certain person, but have allowed fear to creep in. Being obedient can come in many forms, in fact I think it probably looks different for each and every person. So if this speaks to your heart, will you seek to be faithful and do that which God has called you to do?

Trust me from firsthand experience; you'll be glad you did, this is exactly why I wrote another book *"Divine Appointments Revisited!"* It is filled with stories of God's faithfulness when I acted, which sometimes requited me to first *"walk the plank"* so to speak.

Chapter 8

Our response is Crucial!

Ok, so we have come to our final chapter. Chapter four in the book of Jonah and let's start at verse one:

Jonah 4:1-3: Jonah was greatly displeased and became furious.
2 He prayed to the Lord, "Please, Lord, isn't this what I said while I was still in my own country? That's why I fled toward Tarshish in the first place. I knew that you are a gracious and compassionate God, slow to anger, abounding in faithful love, and one who relents from sending disaster.

3 And now, Lord, take my life from me, for it is better for me to die than to live." (CSB Bible)

The Hebrew word here for furious is spot on, it means to be *"glowing hot, or to burn."* Jonah was out of his mind angry, and why? Was it only because God had mercy on a Nation? Let's peel the layers back a bit and gain some insight. A few things were at work here, first, as a Jew, make no doubt about it, Jonah was dealing with a *"nationalistic"* pride. It was an *"I'm so much better than them"* attitude. And when all is said and done in this case, he was probably right because unless you have done a study on the

Assyrians, you can't possibly know that these were evil, wicked and merciless people.

But that still didn't give him the right to be furious. The Scriptures also declare in Romans nine that *"God will have mercy on whom He wills."* Something in general I would think that Jonah would have known. So this nationalistic spirit and holier than thou attitude both played into Jonah's response. So allow me to ask a question...... *"what is keeping you or I from doing what God says?"* Are we holding back from someone because we feel they don't deserve it? Or do the people around you feel inferior to you in your presence by your attitude? Jonah's attitude was so bad that in verse three he actually told God to take his life, that's bad!

Romans 2:11 tells us this: *"For with God there is no partiality."* When I think about Jonah's nationalistic pride, it serves as a reminder to never wrap our Jesus in an American flag, or any other flag for that matter. However, over the last few elections I have witnessed tons of my fellow believers doing that very thing. I recently heard that a new movement has begun of Churches around the country called *"Patriot Church."* I honestly believe this is detrimental to the Good News of the Gospel. The Church getting overly political can only do one thing.......move it away from its lone purpose, to proclaim freedom for those in captivity by sin through the shed blood of Jesus Christ!

This was Jonah's attitude and was definitely part of the reason he ran, he didn't feel these *"pagans"* which they were indeed, didn't deserve God's forgiveness and as we will read, he knew God was going to be merciful. Simply because that is who God is friends!

Chapter 9

Oh to know God

Let's go back and focus in on verse two of chapter four. What an amazing statement from Jonah!

2 He prayed to the Lord, "Please, Lord, isn't this what I said while I was still in my own country? That's why I fled toward Tarshish in the first place. I knew that you are a gracious and compassionate God, slow to anger, abounding in faithful love, and one who relents from sending disaster.

Bingo, there it is! Jonah knew all along what God was going to do and why? Because he no doubt must have seen God do similar things time and time again.

Friends it's who God is, it's what He's renown for. I feel like the lesson of this passage goes hand in hand with the account of Jesus at Simon's house in Luke 7:36-48. In this account, a *"lady of the night,"* perhaps the local call girl if you will run's into Simon the Pharisee's house and falls at the feet of Jesus seeking forgiveness. Here's where these two accounts intersect. Just as the God of Abraham, Isaac and Jacob is renowned for His faithful love, here Jesus is also known for the very same thing!

Stop and think about this......there is NO possible way a lady of the night would ever go near a Pharisee's house, that would the last place on earth she'd ever be found. And if she ever did on her own volition, I have no doubt that the Pharisee would throw her out! But this was Jesus. So there's really only one possible answer as to why she felt comfortable enough to do this. It could only be due to the fact that the word on the street about Jesus was that He was a man of mercy, love and compassion.

And friends, that's who our God is! And nowhere is that made clearer than in the book of Jonah.

God wants to have mercy upon a people that most, if not all other people groups around them would rather see annihilated like Sodom and Gomorrah.

Chapter 10

Do we seek the best for others?

Let's pick up the text in chapter four at verse four as God begins to answer Jonah.

Jonah 4:4-11 The Lord asked, "Is it right for you to be angry?" 5 Jonah left the city and found a place east of it. He made himself a shelter there and sat in its shade to see what would happen to the city. 6 Then the Lord God appointed a plant, and it grew over Jonah to provide shade for his head to rescue him from his trouble. Jonah was greatly pleased with the plant. 7 When dawn came the next day, God appointed a worm that attacked the plant, and it withered. 8 As the sun was rising, God appointed a scorching east wind. The sun beat down on Jonah's head so much that he almost fainted, and he wanted to die. He said, "It's better for me to die than to live."

9 Then God asked Jonah, "Is it right for you to be angry about the plant?" "Yes, it's right!" he replied. "I'm angry enough to die!" 10 And the Lord said, "You cared about the plant, which you did not labor over and did not grow. It appeared in a night and perished in a night. 11 So may I not care about the great city of

Nineveh, which has more than a hundred twenty thousand people who cannot distinguish between their right and their left, as well as many animals?" (CSB Bible)

In verse five we are told that after God questioned him, Jonah outside the city to *"see what would happen."* I truly wonder if when he sat down there was a large part of him that wanted to see fire come down from heaven and consume those Ninevites.

After all, even though he was obedient and we talked previously about how his preaching must have been a sort of halfhearted effort because he wanted them to be annihilated. He's now madder than he's ever been. All of which leads me to ask you a question. *(And frankly myself as I also tell my people "me first!")*

Have you ever found yourself rejoicing or savoring the moment when you hear that an adversary of yours in the flesh has tripped up or has come upon bad circumstances? In the natural it certainly makes one would feel justified doesn't it? But we are told in 1 Corth. 13 that real love which can only come from God. Is a love that never rejoices in the calamity of others friends. I've often shared from my Pulpit something very poignant and powerful. A great test to prove that you've overcome the evil of rejoicing when a person, who has hurt you is when you hear that they are doing well and you rejoice with them in your heart and spirit!

Let's be people, *(me first)* who are not ones to gloat when our fleshly adversaries fall, but rather let's be people who are willing to pray for them, and if and when possible to go the extra mile as Jesus taught and lend them a hand. The eleventh verse in Jonah shows us the unsurpassable compassion of God.......

"So may I not care about the great city of Nineveh, which has more than a hundred twenty thousand people who cannot

distinguish between their right and their left, as well as many animals?" (CSB Bible)

I like what Calvary Chapel Bible teacher Dave Guizak states in his enduring word commentary on this verse:

"The lesson is clear: not only does God's concern for people go beyond Israel, but He is totally justified in calling the nations to account. The lesson of Jonah reminds us that God is the God of all people. The lesson of Jonah is what he proclaimed before being freed from the great fish: Salvation is of the LORD (Jonah 2:9), and not of any race or nation or class. This is the same message God made

clear to Peter in Acts 10:34-35: In truth I perceive that God shows no partiality. But in every nation whoever fears Him and works righteousness is accepted by Him."

What a great truthful proclamation to end this study and chapter with!

Chapter 11

Final Thoughts

First off, thank you for joining me on this journey through one of my favorite books in the Bible. I trust that my prayer at the outset for each of you has been fulfilled via the reading of this book.

I pray that you have learned a lot more about the nature of God. That it is always to save and restore and that judgment is something He takes NO pleasure in dealing out! The Bible is filled with references to restoration like this one in Gal. 6:1a: *Brothers and sisters, if someone is overtaken in any wrongdoing, you who are spiritual, restore such a person with a gentle spirit, watching out for yourselves so that you also won't be tempted.* (CSB Bible)

I also trust you've learned more about the character of God. As with His nature, He seeks to restore and renew whenever possible. I love this deep truth about God that as long as there is even a flicker of hope, He will enter into the situation. I like the way the KJV puts Isaiah 42:3a:

A bruised reed shall he not break, and the smoking flax shall he not quench: he shall bring forth judgment unto truth.

Ever feel bruised or like your life was just a flickering ember, barely alive? If so, know that the God of the entire universe cares!

And last, I pray you have learned a little about His desires. This is the God who desires that *"all mankind should be saved and come into a personal relationship with Him."* (1 Tim. 2:4) So once again, thank you for joining me on this journey and I pray a blessing upon you and yours for all time.

In Christ,

Pastor Al

About the Author

Pastor Al Stewart

Makes his home in Ormond Beach, Fl. with his wife Dawn. He has 2 sons as well as a stepson. Al has pastored for over 30+ years and has planted some 4 Churches and currently serves as the Senior Pastor of Greater Grace Chapel of Daytona Beach. *(ggcdaytona.com)* He is a native of Waterbury, Ct. and attended Golden State School of Theology and Schofield Seminary later earning an Honorary Doctorate from Adonai International Christian University *[A.I.C.U.]* for his Apologetics work among Jehovah's Witnesses and Latter Day Saints. Pastor Al is also an ordained Police/Fire Chaplain through Shield of Faith Ministries and is was ordained through Adonai International Fellowship Alliance *[A.I.F.A.]* and served as the Chaplain of Post 16 American Legion of Lynchburg, Va. He served in the U.S. Army from 1977-80 in West Germany. He has appeared on TBN's *"Praise the Lord"* program as well as the Midwest Outreach

Podcast, and many other programs. Al is available on occasion to speak. He can be reached at:

PoBoy Publishing
125 Hidden Hills Dr.
Ormond Beach, Fl. 32174 *(email: rev.stew@outlook.com)*

Additional Books Available by Pastor Al Stewart through PoBoy Publishing:

"Works Revisited"
(Amazon/KDP)

"The Watchtower Revisited, Dangerous Doctrines of Jehovah's Witnesses"
(Amazon/KDP)

"The Importance of Just One Revisited" (Amazon/KDP)

"Mormonism Revisited" (Amazon/KDP)

"How to share Jesus Effectively" (Amazon/KDP)

"Wendy, Beauty From Ashes" (Amazon/KDP)

"East Germany Revisited, Utopia Failed" (Amazon/KDP)

"Wesleyan-Arminian Theology Revisited" (Amazon/KDP)

"Put Your Hand's Up, Arrested by God, Atheist Cop Comes to Christ" Testimony of Officer Bob Faubel, A PoBoy Publication (Amazon/KDP)

"Divine Appointments Revisited"
(Amazon/KDP)

"UFOs Revisited, What can we know for Sure?"
(Amazon/KDP)

"What Matters Most, In the Christian Life"
(Amazon/KDP)

"Jesus Revisited, Never accept a Counterfeit"
(Amazon/KDP)

Leave A Review!

In choosing to be a self-publisher, I can't tell you how important leaving a good review is!

Simply type in the book title on Amazon to find the book's page and click on "*leave a review,*" it's that's simple and thank you in advance!   - Pastor Al

www.ingramcontent.com/pod-product-compliance
Lightning Source LLC
LaVergne TN
LVHW010501160826
845677LV00012B/2590
9798844162121